PRACTICAL ECONOMICS

A TEEN GUIDE TO

Saving and
INVESTING

Tammy
Gagne

Mitchell Lane
PUBLISHERS
P.O. Box 196
Hockessin, Delaware 19707

PRACTICAL ECONOMICS FOR TEENS

A Teen Guide to Buying Goods and Services
A Teen Guide to Earning Income
A Teen Guide to Protecting and Insuring Assets
A Teen Guide to Saving and Investing

Copyright © 2014 by Mitchell Lane Publishers

DISCLAIMER: Mitchell Lane Publishers is not
a securities advisor. The views here belong
solely to the author and should not be used or
considered as investment advice. Individuals
must determine the suitability for their own
situation and perform their own due diligence
before making any investment or financial
decision.

ABOUT THE AUTHOR: Tammy Gagne has
authored dozens of books for both adults
and children over the last decade. Several of
her titles, including A Dividend Stock Strategy
for Teens and A Teen Guide to Safe-Haven
Savings for Mitchell Lane Publishers, focus on
finances. Teaching her own teenage son to be
a savvy consumer has long been one of her
biggest priorities. She thinks all young people
should understand how the economy works. By
striking a balance between shrewd saving and
conscious spending, teens can become the
change that is needed in our economy.

Printing 1 2 3 4 5 6 7 8 9

Library of Congress
Cataloging-in-Publication Data
Gagne, Tammy.
 A teen guide to saving and investing / by
Tammy Gagne.
    pages cm. — (Practical economics for
teens)
 Audience: Grade 4 to 8
 Includes bibliographical references and index.
 ISBN 978-1-61228-471-2 (library bound)
 1. Finance, Personal—Juvenile literature.
 2. Saving and investment—Juvenile literature.
 I. Title.
 HG179.G2344 2013
 332.02400835—dc23
                                    2013023030
eBook ISBN: 9781612285276
                                    PLB

CONTENTS

CHAPTER 1

Finding Money to
SAVE

You have probably heard people say that money makes the world go 'round. This common phrase is a bit of an exaggeration. After all, it doesn't take a dime to make the Earth spin on its axis. It does take money to do nearly everything else that happens in the world, though. We use money to meet our everyday needs like food, shelter, and clothing. We also need money to improve our lives with things like good health care, college educations, and homes of our own. Saving money is the first step towards meeting these larger financial goals.

Many people mistakenly believe that it takes a large amount of money to make saving and investing worthwhile. They think that without a sizeable chunk of cash to put away all at once, they won't be able to grow their savings quickly enough. The truth is that the best way to grow your money is to start saving while you are young. If you make saving a habit today, you will have considerably more money later.

But where does the money come from? If you earn an allowance, this weekly payment—however small it is—is an excellent starting point. If you babysit, mow lawns, or shovel snow for a few dollars here and there, these earnings can also help add to your savings. If you have a regular part-time job, you are in the perfect position to start your savings plan.

The first "job" that many kids have is doing chores around the house for their parents. The amount of money you get weekly from your allowance might not seem like much. Put this money into a savings account each week, though, and it can add up surprisingly quickly.

All you need is a strategy to turn this regular income into an investment for your future.

The best way to make sure that you save money is to do it when you get paid. As soon as you get your paycheck or your allowance money, head straight to the bank. Decide on a specific amount of money to save each week or month. A great way to balance your spending and saving is to save half of every dollar you make. If you can't save half, try saving at least 25 percent. Saving money regularly is more important than the exact amount you are putting away.

What if you have no job or allowance? What if your parents pay for all your needs and give you money for the occasional things that you want? Finding money to save may seem like a challenge in this situation, but you may be surprised how much money you can save by taking a look at your spending habits. How much money do you spend every day, every week, and every month? Saving money begins with spending less. Once you find ways to cut back on spending, you can then deposit the money you aren't spending into a savings account or other investment.

For example, do you buy your breakfast or lunch most days? Do you buy water, soft drinks, or snacks from vending machines or convenience stores? If so, you could save half of the money you are spending on these items by making a few simple changes in your routine. Begin by eating breakfast at home each morning. Next, take a sandwich or another healthy meal to school with you each day. Water is healthy, but why should you buy bottled water when you can fill a reusable bottle at home each morning? Soft drinks and snack foods are not only expensive, but they are also bad for your health. Brown bagging it and skipping the vending machine could save you $50 a month or more.[1]

If your parents deposit money into your school lunch account each month, ask them if they would be willing to let

Eating breakfast at home each morning can help you save money two ways. First, you will save the money you would have spent on buying your breakfast elsewhere. Second, if you are willing to cook for the rest of your family, your parents just might be willing to raise your allowance to pay you for this added chore.

you manage the cash instead. Many people spend far more money when they can simply swipe a debit card through a machine than when they have to dole out cold hard cash. You may save money by simply thinking more about what you are buying. This is especially true if your school offers a la carte lunches. Buying a cookie to go with your lunch each day may be fun in the moment, but you could save an additional $15 a month just by skipping this sugary snack. If you must have cookies with your lunches, consider baking them at home. It's much cheaper, and often tastier, this way.

Also, consider how often you go out to eat with your family. According to a recent study by Rutgers University, the average family spends 40 percent of its budget on eating out.[2] Cutting down on eating at restaurants is one of the easiest ways most families can save money. Eating at home is less expensive and usually healthier than eating out as well. Imagine how much money you could help your parents save by coming up with a new meal strategy. They may even be willing to share some of the wealth.

If you don't get an allowance for doing chores now, you may be able to convince your parents to give you one by offering to save them money. Ask if they would be willing to give you $10 a week (or $10 more, if you already receive an allowance) if you can save them $20 each week. Chances are good that your parents will appreciate that you are thinking of the family budget. At the very least, your offer may intrigue them enough to accept your challenge.

If you currently eat out two or three nights a week, you can save at least $20 by eliminating just one of these outings. Perhaps you could cook dinner on this night of the week instead. You might even decide to limit eating out to only once a week. Want to save even more? Get takeout food instead of sitting down to dinner at a restaurant on that one night. The food will be less expensive, you won't have to buy drinks, and you won't have to leave a tip.

Explain to your parents that you plan to save the extra money they give you, and suggest they do the same with the money they aren't spending on eating out. Even after they raise your allowance, they will still be saving more than $1,000 a year by making these changes. If they put this money into an individual retirement account (IRA), they could turn this small amount of money into more than $45,000

Saving and Investing Tips and Trivia

If you find yourself spending money often, try this savings trick: Each time you buy something, round the expense up to the nearest dollar and save the difference. Let's say that you go to the mall and spend $12.75 on a gift for a friend's birthday—you would round up to $13 and save the extra $0.25. If you also spend $2.25 on a slice of pizza and a drink for lunch, and $10.50 on a new t-shirt for yourself, then you would save a total of $1.50. It might not seem like much money at first, but over time this strategy can really add to your savings.

in the next twenty years, assuming an 8 percent annual return. If you put your $10 a week in an IRA* of your own, and continue to invest just $10 a week over the next fifty years, you could turn your money into nearly $300,000.[3]

Certainly, cutting back on eating out isn't the only way you can find money for savings. You can also save money by reducing your spending in numerous other ways. To find out exactly where your money is going, keep a journal of every cent you spend over the next month. At the end of the month, consider every item you bought. Ask yourself the following questions: Did you really need it? Was there a less expensive option available? Was there another way to get the item altogether? For example, instead of buying new clothes for a special occasion, could you have borrowed an outfit from a friend? Could you have found the new book or movie that you bought at your local library instead? You might be amazed at the number of ways you can save money if you just take the time to consider all your options.

*You must have W2 wages to save money in an IRA.

If you want to make some extra cash, consider a part-time job. Here are just a few popular jobs for teens:

- Camp counselor
- Clothing store clerk
- Golf caddy
- Grocery store cashier
- Lifeguard or swim instructor
- Newspaper delivery person
- Pet sitter or dog walker
- Pizza delivery person
- Restaurant host or hostess
- Restaurant server
- Tutor
- Warehouse stocker
- Website designer

Tutoring is a great way to make extra cash.

Starting
SMALL

When you get into the habit of saving, you want to hold on to as much of your money as you can. If you are keeping your cash at home, though, you are missing out on a very important benefit of the saving process: interest. This is the money that your savings can earn by placing it in a savings account or other type of investment. The interest the bank pays you is based on the amount of money you keep in your account. Let's say that you place your savings in an account that pays 1 percent APY (annual percentage yield)*. If you deposit $100 and keep it there for one year, you will make $1 in interest. If you deposit $500, you will have an extra $5 after one year.

Piggy banks are great for collecting and saving loose change. As soon as you have enough coins to roll up and deposit, though, putting them in the bank is the smarter option. Keeping large amounts of cash at home can be risky. What if you misplace your money? Keeping your cash where you can get to it quickly can also make it more tempting for you to spend it. You may think twice about spending your savings if you have to make a trip to the bank to withdraw it.

*Interest rates are for illustration purposes only and may not be representative of rates that are actually available at the time you are reading this book.

It is much harder to spend money if you have to make a special trip to the bank to withdraw it first. In the time it takes you to get to the bank, you might decide that you really don't want to spend your hard-earned savings after all.

SAVINGS DEPOSIT

	CASH	
	CHECKS	
	TOTAL FROM OTHER SIDE	
	CASH RETURNED	
	TOTAL	

ACCOUNT NUMBER (10 DIGITS)
TELLER: PRINT TRANSACTION ON LINE 7

ID REQUIRED FOR CASH BACK
☐ PIN ☐ CC w/PIN ☐ DL OR ID# _____

_____
CUSTOMER SIGNATURE (CASH RETURNED)

When you deposit money into your bank account, you may need to fill out a deposit slip. Checks must be listed separately on this form, along with any cash that you are depositing. It is also important to get a receipt when you make a deposit. Keep this item with your other bank records.

If you don't already have a savings account, now is the time to open one. Many teenagers simply open an account with the bank where their parents do business. Before you go this route, do a little research. Interest rates vary widely from one bank to another. The internet can be a very helpful tool in finding the bank that will offer you the highest interest rate on your savings. Websites like Bankrate.com and BestRates.com offer lists of the bank accounts with the highest APYs.

It's also wise to do some local research. Oftentimes credit unions offer the best interest rates on savings accounts. You have to belong to one of these member-owned institutions to open an account, but the requirements are usually pretty

simple. Many credit unions are open to residents of a particular community. Others serve people who work in a certain profession. You may also be able to open your own account at a credit union that one of your parents is a member of. If you are a minor, you will need a parent to co-sign your account no matter where you open it.

One of the biggest advantages of doing business with a credit union is that they typically charge fewer fees on their accounts. Many charge none at all. Credit unions often have lower minimum balance requirements than many banks do, as well. A bank may require you to keep $100 or possibly even more in your savings at all times. If your balance dips below this amount, the bank will charge you a fee each month until the balance returns to the minimum amount. If you're not careful, this monthly fee could empty your savings account. Minimum balances to avoid a fee are usually lower with a savings account at a credit union, however. Many credit unions (and even some banks) have no minimum balance at all.

A regular savings account, or statement savings account, is the most basic form of investment. It is called a statement savings account because you will receive regular statements that list all activity on the account. Deposits, withdrawals, fees, and interest will all be included on this paperwork. Some banks send out monthly statements; others only issue statements quarterly for savings accounts. You can also opt to have your statements sent to you electronically instead of having paper copies mailed to you.

In between statements, many people use online banking to manage their accounts. Once you have set up a password, you can access your account twenty-four hours a day, seven days a week from your computer. Checking your account online is a great way to watch your interest grow. Some banks and credit unions even allow you to make deposits

electronically. Certainly, you cannot deposit cash into your account without making a trip to the bank. But you can use a smartphone application to snap photos of checks to deposit them into an account that offers this convenient feature. Some savings accounts only allow you to make up to six "convenient" withdrawals a month (including phone and internet transfers, automatic transfers, and payments by check or debit card). Some banks or credit unions allow even fewer withdrawals, and will charge fees if you exceed those limits. Accounts that offer free unlimited withdrawals can be found, however, provided that any withdrawals that exceed six per month are made in person or at an ATM. If you cannot find such an account and need to make frequent withdrawals, it is smarter to keep your money in a low- or no-fee checking account.

As long as your bank or credit union is insured by the Federal Deposit Insurance Corporation (FDIC),your money is completely safe. Even if the bank is robbed or goes bankrupt, the FDIC will insure up to $250,000 per person.[1] Before your balance gets even close to this amount, however, you should consider moving some of your savings into an investment that offers you a better return. Statement savings are a great way to start. They are also an ideal place to save for short-term goals. Compared to other investments, though, statement savings offer the lowest potential for growth.

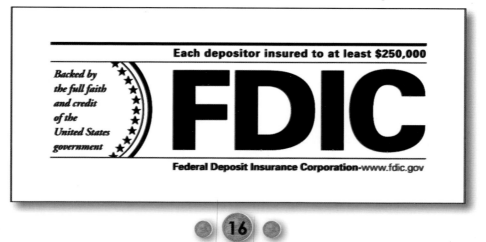

Each depositor insured to at least $250,000

Backed by the full faith and credit of the United States government

FDIC

Federal Deposit Insurance Corporation-www.fdic.gov

Be sure to look over your bank account statement each month or quarter as soon as it arrives. Compare the deposits and withdrawal amounts you recorded in your bank register to the ones listed on this document. Add any interest you have earned to the balance in your register at this time.

By now you have already learned not to spend your money on unnecessary items. It is also important that you take advantage of every opportunity to earn as much interest as possible on your savings. Let's say that you have been saving $25 a week for a whole year. Your savings account now has a balance of $1,300. If you are earning 1 percent interest, you will earn $13 on this money over the next year with a statement savings account. If you moved $1,275 into a one-year certificate of deposit (CD), you might be able to earn 1.15 percent. You would earn $14.66 instead.

Saving and Investing Tips and Trivia

When opening a savings account, ask whether the bank offers any special savings programs or rewards for young people. Some institutions hold drawings for cash or prizes each month to underage savers. For example, you might receive one entry just for being an account holder and another for each deposit you make that month. You also might be able to earn rewards by referring new customers. Some banks offer a cash reward for every new account that you bring to the company.

Like savings accounts, CDs pay you interest. But with a CD, you are required to keep a certain amount of money in the bank for a certain amount of time. You may choose to invest your money in a CD for any number of years—from one to ten. You can even find certificates of deposit that only require a three-, six-, or nine-month commitment. If you withdraw your money early, you will usually pay a fee called a penalty. Depending on the terms of the CD, you could lose part or all of your interest, but you won't lose your original investment. This amount is called the principal.

You might think the extra $1.66 you could make from a CD isn't much money. Not taking advantage of the higher interest rate, however, is like throwing money away. Consider what you would do right now if someone handed you $1.66 in cash. Picture the dollar bill, two quarters, dime, nickel, and penny. Would you toss this money into the trash? Of course not! So why would you pass up the opportunity to earn even this small amount more on your savings?

If you want to make more money with a CD, all you have to do is agree to keep it for a longer period of time. That one-year CD may have only offered 1.15 percent interest, but a five-year CD might offer 1.8 percent. Five years is a

much longer commitment than one, though, so it is important that you will not need access to this money during that time.

Another safe investment for long-term savings is a savings bond. This investment is offered by the United States government through the TreasuryDirect website: www.treasurydirect.gov. A savings bond works a lot like a loan. When someone borrows money from a bank, the bank requires that person to pay back the amount borrowed plus interest. When you buy a savings bond, though, you are loaning money to the government. In this case you are the one who receives the interest when the loan is repaid. Savings bonds earn interest for up to thirty years.[2] When a bond stops earning interest, it is said to have matured.

You must keep a savings bond for at least twelve months before redeeming it. You can cash it in after that, but if you do so before five years have passed, you will pay a penalty. As with a CD, you won't lose your principal in this situation. You will simply lose the last three months of interest that the bond has earned.[3] You should only buy savings bonds if you intend to keep them for several years. Ideally, you will want to keep them until they mature, so they can earn as much interest as possible. If, however, interest rates rise or you are able to earn a higher yield with another investment, it may be worth cashing in early.

Saving and Investing Tips and Trivia

If you want to buy $500 worth of CDs, consider laddering your investment. Instead of putting all your money into a single CD, buy five separate CDs that mature over different time periods. If you need money, this strategy makes it easier to get part of your cash without paying penalties on the entire amount. If your timing is right, you may not have to pay a penalty at all.

CHAPTER 3

Exploring More
SAVINGS OPTIONS

Statement savings accounts and CDs are wonderful first steps to saving. If you are interested in long-term savings, though, it is smart to consider investments that will offer you a higher yield. Some of these options will only be available to you once you have put away a certain amount of cash. As soon as you have the minimum amount, you may want to think about moving most of your money into one or more of these higher-yield investments.

Money market accounts work a lot like regular savings accounts. You can open either type of account at a bank or credit union. Just like a savings account, the number of withdrawals you can make from a money market account each month has certain limits. But a money market account has a much higher minimum balance requirement. You will likely need several thousand dollars to open this type of account.

Because you keep more money in a money market account, the bank can pay you a higher interest rate for this type of account. It is important to consider all the details before signing up, though. Compared to other long-term investments, the interest you make from a money market account may still be pretty low. The interest and minimum balances will also differ from one institution to another.

A credit union may ask that you keep only $2,500 in your money market account. This might seem like a great deal

Deciding how to invest a large amount of money may feel a bit overwhelming at first. Take some time to learn about all your options before making your choice. You can even place your money into several smaller investments if you prefer.

when most banks are asking for minimum balances of $10,000 or more. Be sure to read the fine print, though. The credit union's money market account may allow you to start with only $2,500, but it may not pay the higher interest rate (or any interest at all) until you reach a much higher balance.

Also, be sure to ask about fees. The bank may pay you a higher interest rate on a money market account, but the service fees the institution charges may mean that you don't make any more money than you would have with a regular savings account. You could even end up with less money by choosing this type of account. Unless you have a large amount of money, a money market account may not benefit you at this point in your life. And even if you do have a large amount of money, it may be smarter to put it into an investment that offers a higher return.

Savings accounts and CDs are the safest places to keep your money. Even money market accounts are among this safe-haven group of investments. Not only are you guaranteed not to lose any of your principal, but you also know exactly how much interest your money will earn. These investments are safe and predictable, which is why they offer the lowest amounts of interest. If you are willing to place some of your money into medium-risk investments, you will have the potential to earn more money. It must be said, though, that you will also have the potential to lose some or all of your money.

Deciding to move even a small amount of money into medium-risk investments can be difficult for many people. You have probably grown up hearing people say that it is better to be safe than sorry. Certainly, this saying may apply to your savings. You might prefer to have $1,000 safely in the bank, earning a promised $10 a year rather than to risk losing part or all of your money while trying to earn more. The good thing about medium-risk investments is that the chances of

losing all your money with them is still fairly low. At the same time, you have a much better chance of increasing your wealth more quickly with one of these options.

One way to earn more interest without increasing your risk too much is buying bonds. Savings bonds are only one type of bond available to investors. If you like the idea of investing in the United States government, you can also buy three other types of government investments. Treasury bills, Treasury notes, and Treasury bonds all offer fixed interest rates, but each of them takes a different amount of time to mature, or reach their face value. Treasury bills, often called T-bills, mature within one year. You can buy a Treasury note that will mature in two, three, five, seven, or ten years. The longest-term Treasury investment is the Treasury bond, which is available only for a thirty-year term.[1]

These investments also work a bit differently than regular savings bonds. When you purchase a savings bond, you pay its face value. This means that a $100 savings bond costs $100. The interest you earn is added to this amount. Treasury

Saving and Investing Tips and Trivia

Over time, the cost of most goods and services increases. This rise in the general price level is called inflation. Many of the safest investments don't pay enough interest to keep up with inflation. So even though your bank balance is growing, the new larger amount buys less than the smaller amount did a year ago. For investors who want to combat this but still keep their risk low, the US Treasury offers two investments that compensate for changes in the Consumer Price Index. Treasury Inflation-Protected Securities, or TIPS, are purchased at auction or through a reseller just like Treasury bills, notes, and bonds, but the principal amount of the investment is adjusted as the Consumer Price Index changes. I Bonds are savings bonds that pay interest based on the rate of inflation.

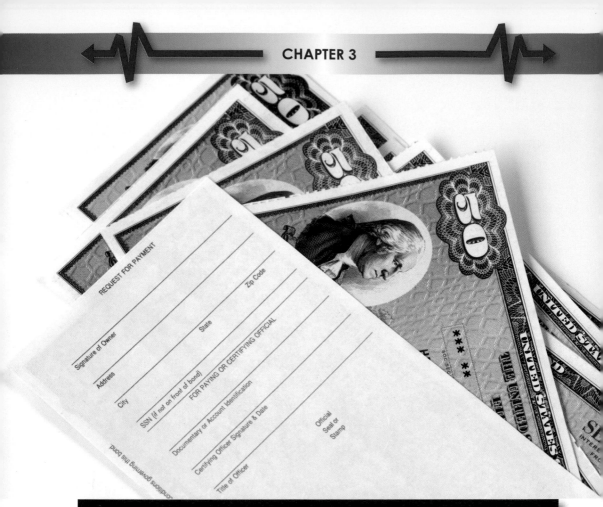

Regular savings bonds cannot be purchased or sold on the secondary market. When you buy a savings bond, you must keep it for at least a year before redeeming it. Ideally, you want to keep it much longer than this to take advantage of all the interest it can earn.

bills, notes, and bonds are sold at Treasury auctions, often for less than their face value. They also pay interest to the investor every six months, and then are redeemed for face value at maturity. Even though Treasuries can be bought at auction, most people buy them on the secondary market. Banks and brokerage firms buy these investments at auction and then resell them to their clients.

Whether or not a Treasury investment ends up being a good one depends on how much you pay for it. If you can get them for a low enough price, you can earn good returns on Treasuries. If you pay too much, you will make less from this investment. How profitable your investment turns out to be also depends on the economy and changes in interest rates. Let's say that you buy a ten-year Treasury note today. If interest rates stay the same, you could make a fair amount of money. If interest rates on investments go up over the next decade, though, you may end up wishing you hadn't committed your money to this lower-paying investment.

No one knows for sure where interest rates are going to go over the next ten years. It is impossible to say for certain what will happen even in the next twelve months. In general, though, it is easier to predict short-term changes in the economy. For this reason T-bills are considered the safest type of Treasury investment.

Another advantage to Treasuries is that you can sell them. This trait makes these investments more liquid than savings bonds. A liquid investment is one that you can redeem or sell quickly if you need access to cash. Remember, a savings bond cannot be redeemed for the first twelve months after purchasing it, and you will lose your last three months' worth of interest if you do so within the first five years. You can lose money when you sell Treasuries as well, but it is also possible to make money.

Another way to invest in the government is by buying municipal bonds. These investments are issued by local governments to help pay for projects like building schools and roads. Certain companies that provide a public service— such as utility companies—may also issue municipal bonds. One type of government bonds issued by cities, counties, and states is a general obligation bond. The interest paid on

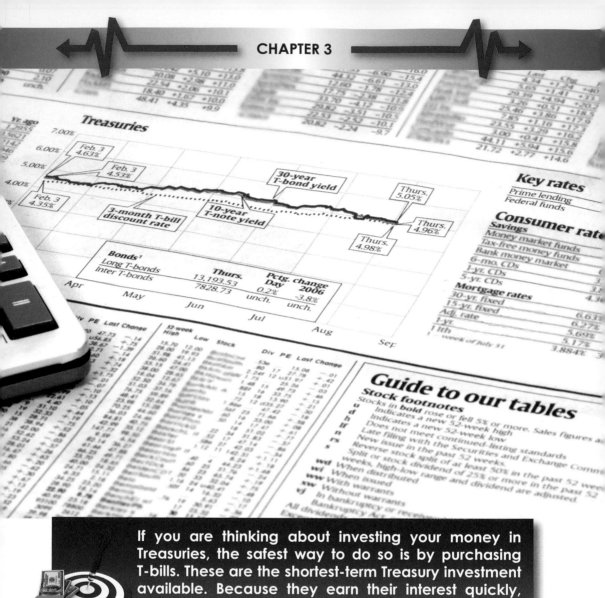

If you are thinking about investing your money in Treasuries, the safest way to do so is by purchasing T-bills. These are the shortest-term Treasury investment available. Because they earn their interest quickly, there is less risk of rates changing too much before T-bills mature.

these bonds usually comes from taxes. Revenue bonds can be issued by either governments or companies and are paid back with the money the company or government makes from the project.

Municipal bonds offer an overwhelming advantage over many other investment types: They are virtually tax-free. You will not have to pay federal income tax on the money you

make from a municipal bond.[2] As long as you live in the state where the bond is issued, you probably won't have to pay any state or local taxes on your earnings either. If you are just beginning to invest, taxes may not be a big concern for you. Once your savings start growing, however, saving money on taxes becomes another important way to make the most of your money.

Municipal bonds are considered medium-risk investments. Although you are very likely to get your money back with interest in most cases, it is possible for you to lose any or all of your money. You must consider this risk before investing. You can lessen your risk by choosing your municipal bond wisely. General obligation bonds are usually less risky because the government that issues them promises to pay them back regardless of whether they earn money from the investment or not. The government can raise taxes if necessary to pay these bonds back. Revenue bonds are paid back only from the money the project earns. When buying general obligation bonds, states, cities, and towns that repeatedly manage to balance their budgets are the best risks. If you are buying revenue bonds, look for municipalities or companies with proven track records as well. New companies may be more likely to default, or not repay the money they owe.

Saving and Investing Tips and Trivia

Junior Achievement is a nonprofit youth organization that teaches kids about economics and finance. Ask your teacher or principal if your school has a Junior Achievement volunteer. You can also visit www.ja.org for more information about the programs offered by this group.

CHAPTER 4

Risks and REWARDS

As most financial experts will tell you, it is important to diversify your savings. This means placing your money in different investments. These can be different investments of the same type (for example, two different municipal bonds), but you should also include different types of investments, such as municipal bonds and CDs. If you put all of your money in no- or low-risk investments, you will not grow your savings to its full potential. On the other hand, if you put all of your money into high-risk investments, you take the chance of losing all your savings. Medium-risk investments may seem like a great happy medium, but the truth is that putting all your money into any one type of investment is usually a bad idea. The best savings plan is one that includes all of these choices.

The exact amount of money you choose to place in low-, medium-, and high-risk investments is up to you (and your parents, of course). Perhaps you simply aren't comfortable with high-risk investments. You should never place any amount of money that you cannot afford to lose into any investment that isn't guaranteed—period. If you are in a position to take on a bit of risk, however, it could pay off by adding to your savings substantially.

If you like the idea of buying bonds, but you aren't thrilled about the low returns municipal bonds offer, consider

Stocks offer good potential as investments. It is important to do careful research, however. How long has the company been in business? How is the industry in general doing right now? Check your newspaper for a list of the most popular stocks and their current share prices.

corporate bonds instead. These bonds are issued by private companies and offer higher interest rates. It is important to understand that the risk is also higher with these investments. In fact, the higher the interest rate, the bigger the risk may be.[1] How risky a corporate bond is depends on the company that issues it.

Any business can fail at any time; if this happens, there is a chance that it will not be able to repay its loans, including bonds. There are no guarantees, but a company that has been around for a long time and is doing just as well now as it was twenty years ago may present less of a risk. Each

At one time most publicly traded companies issued stock certificates to their shareholders. Today, however, most stockholders simply receive statements that list how many shares they own and how much each share made in dividends since the last statement was issued.

company also has a credit rating. The best of these is AAA. Investment-grade ratings (those that are considered the safest) then go down to AA, A, and BBB. The lower the rating, the greater risk there is. You may have heard of junk bonds. These are bonds that offer very high rates of interest, but they come with extremely high risk as well. Junk bonds have credit ratings of BB and lower.

Another type of investment on the higher-risk side of investing is stocks. Despite the risks, stocks in general have outperformed every other type of investment in history over time.[2] Stocks are similar to corporate bonds in that they are sold by companies. When you purchase stock, though, you are actually buying a very small piece of the company called a share. When a company performs well, its stock value generally goes up. If the company doesn't do well, its stock value drops. Public opinion of a company and speculation about its future might also cause a stock to trade

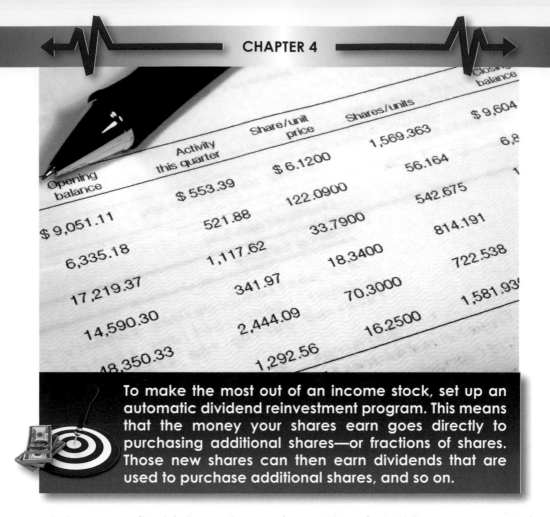

Opening balance	Activity this quarter	Share/unit price	Shares/units	Closing balance
			1,569.363	$9,604
		$6.1200	56.164	6,8
	$553.39	122.0900	542.675	1
$9,051.11	521.88	33.7900	814.191	
6,335.18	1,117.62	18.3400	722.538	
17,219.37	341.97	70.3000	1,581.93	
14,590.30	2,444.09	16.2500		
18,350.33	1,292.56			

To make the most out of an income stock, set up an automatic dividend reinvestment program. This means that the money your shares earn goes directly to purchasing additional shares—or fractions of shares. Those new shares can then earn dividends that are used to purchase additional shares, and so on.

at temporarily high or low prices. The first thing you must decide when investing in stock is whether you are looking for a growth stock, a value stock, or an income stock. Investors interested in growth want to buy low and sell high. They may not be looking at the investment as a short-term one, but they may sell if the price skyrockets in a short period of time.

Growth stocks are usually young companies that are expected to expand and become more profitable over time. If this happens, the value of each share should also increase. Let's say you buy $500 worth of shares in a company whose stock is selling for $20 a share today. You might hold on to the stock for an entire year before you see it increase. During this time you may even see it drop occasionally. By the second year, though, you might notice a sharp spike in

Saving and Investing Tips and Trivia

You don't have to be a customer of a certain company to invest in it, but it doesn't hurt. Make a point of paying attention to the products you and your friends buy the most. Also watch your parents to see where they spend their money. If your friends and family members are buying certain brands over and over, these might be good options for a stock investment.

its value. What do you do when you wake up one morning to find out that your stock is now worth $50 a share? This means that your original investment of $500 is now worth $1,250. You could opt to hold onto your shares to see if they increase any more. Or you could sell them all right then and there. No one will know for sure which is the better decision until time has passed and the stock either increases or decreases in value.

Keep in mind, though, that if the company doesn't do as well as you thought it would, you could find that your stock is worth $5 per share after a year instead of $50. Your $500 investment would now be worth only $125. What would you do in this situation? You could sell to avoid losing any more money, or you could stay put to see whether the value will eventually recover.

Another strategy that stock investors use is value investing. Value investors look for stocks that they believe are undervalued—selling for less than what they're actually worth. Maybe the entire banking industry is not doing well. Even a strong bank's stock trading price could drop below what it's actually worth if investors are afraid of owning stock in any bank at all. The value investor's strategy is to hold

onto these stocks hoping that their prices will increase to their true value once the banking industry's problems have passed.

Not everyone buys stocks to make such incredible gains. In reality, large, rapid increases in stock value are rare. Many investors prefer to buy income stocks for this reason. Like growth stocks, income stocks are constantly rising or falling in value. When your stock value increases, you can certainly sell the stock to make a profit, but there is also a benefit to holding onto the stock. Income stocks pay dividends. These monthly or quarterly payments are based on the number of shares you own. The more shares you own, the higher your dividend payment will be. Not all companies offer dividends, so if this is important to you, do your research to make sure that the company you choose does.

People who invest large amounts of money in stocks can make a lot of money from dividends. Even if you only invest a small amount of your savings in stocks, you can make the most of this investment by reinvesting your dividends. A dividend reinvestment program (DRP or DRIP) automatically puts the money you make through dividends back into additional stock purchases. Your dividends for one month or

Saving and Investing Tips and Trivia

Since you will need an adult to help you make a stock purchase, consider asking your parents if they would be willing to be your partners in the investment. Perhaps you only make $40 a month from your allowance, but you need $50 a month to buy a certain stock. Maybe your parents would be willing to invest the remaining $10. If they say yes, just remember that 20 percent of the total investment belongs to them.

quarter may not be enough to buy a whole share. When this is the case, partial shares will be purchased. You might not think that you will grow a small investment much this way, but remember that those partial shares will be earning you even more dividends the next time around.

Many people who invest in stocks use brokers, or sales agents. You can find several different websites that allow you to buy and sell stocks electronically for a small fee. You can also purchase this type of investment on your own if you prefer. Numerous companies offer direct stock purchase plans (DSPPs). You can check to see if a particular company offers one of these plans, or you can browse listings of companies that offer DSPPs on the websites of companies such as First Share or Moneypaper.

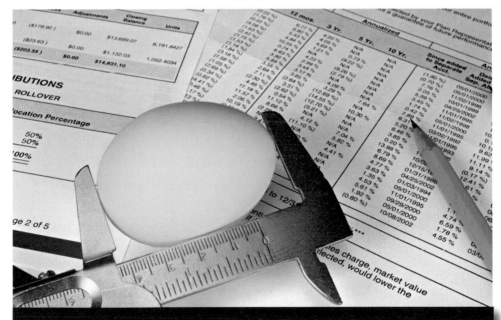

You probably won't strike it rich with any single investment. You may even lose a little money on one stock or another. Over time, though, putting your long-term savings in a variety of investments can help you build a sizeable nest egg for the future.

Each company has its own minimum purchase price for its stock. Some companies may require new investors to buy $500 worth of stock or more. Others have minimums as low as $50. If you want to buy a stock with a high minimum, check to see if the company waives the minimum requirement for investors who agree to buy stock monthly. Many plans with a $500 minimum, for example, will allow new investors to work toward this amount over time. A plan like this might ask that you agree to invest $50 each month for the next ten months. You won't need to send the company your money each month; you simply sign paperwork that allows the company to make an automatic monthly deduction from your bank account.

Many times buying stock this way works out better than if you had purchased your stock all at once. Let's say you start an automatic deduction in January by investing $25. Meanwhile another investor buys $250 worth of stock at the same time. If the stock is worth $25 a share on this day, you will begin by owning one share. The other investor will start out owning ten shares.

Now let's say that the price per share drops $3 each month for the next four months. By May you will have invested $125 for a total 6.94 shares. The other investor will have invested $250 for a total of 10 shares. Now let's say that the stock starts going up $3 each month for the next five months. By October you will have invested $250 for a total of 12.85 shares. The other investor has still only invested $250, but for a total of only 10 shares. You will have almost 30 percent more stock for the exact same price. This advantage to investing over time is called dollar cost averaging.

No one can say whether a stock will go up, down, or stay the same while you own it. Like almost everything else with stocks, there is no guarantee that you will make out better buying over time. But even if the stock price in the example

Ending
Balance
(12/31/06)

.52
18
32
6
7
5

$5,827.20
5,930.98
37,192.75
35,573.31
38,298.91
$122,823.15

How your ending balance was distributed
as of 12/31/06 (see pie chart):

Individual Fund(s)

G Fund
F Fund
C Fund
S Fund
I Fund

5%
5%
30%
29%
31%

g balance is
the funds

Portfolio Summary

Current Value

$13,937

$14,014

$77

$13,937

.014

Picking successful mutual funds isn't for amateurs. It is best to consult an experienced financial planner if you are interested in these investments. He or she can direct you towards the best options for your savings goals.

above had remained the same over the ten months, your investment would have been worth no less than the other investor's.

Another way to lessen the risk involved in buying stocks is to invest in mutual funds. These investments are made up of many different stocks, bonds, and other investments. If one investment does poorly, several others may do well enough to make up the loss. Mutual funds are still considered high-risk investments. Choosing the best ones can be just as difficult as picking good stocks, perhaps even more so. For this reason it may be best to use a financial planner when buying this kind of investment.

Financing Your DREAMS

Saving for the future may not sound as exciting as putting money away for a new laptop computer or a car. You might think it is much too early to think about saving for things like buying your first home or retiring. Maybe having a fancy house or a lavish lifestyle is not important to you. By saving just a little money now, though, you can help make sure you never have to worry about having enough money for the things you need.

One of the best parts of saving, in fact, is earning interest on the money you put away. Even better, though, is earning compound interest. Put simply, this is the interest that your interest earns. When you start saving while you are young, compound interest can make all the difference in your savings totals. As a teenager you have time on your side.

Let's say that you begin putting $100 a month into an individual retirement account (IRA)* at the age of fifteen. If you continued doing this until you retired at age sixty-five, and you earned an average return of 8 percent per year, you would have more than $688,000.[1] Now let's say that you don't start thinking about retirement until you are fifty-five. By this time you will probably be making much more money. You might even be able to put the maximum amount into your IRA. The limit for 2013 is $5,500 a year, or $458.33 per

*To contribute to an IRA, you must earn W2 wages.

Many students need to borrow money in order to go to college. Paying back these student loans after graduation can be difficult for any young person. By saving money for college today, you can lessen the amount you may need to borrow for school later.

CHAPTER 5

Saving and Investing Tips and Trivia

The more time you have until you will need money from your investments, the more risks you can afford to take. Both college and retirement savings plans include investments like bonds, stocks, and even cash investments. Discuss the type of investments in your plan with your financial planner. If you won't need the money for a while, you can afford to invest more money in high-risk investments like stock. As you get closer to the time when you need your money, ask that more of the money be moved into bonds and cash savings.

month. If you went this route instead, you would end up with less than $80,000 at the age of sixty-five—a little more than a tenth of what you could have had by starting earlier.[2]

Another benefit to starting an IRA now is that you can use some of the money you put away for your education. The first big expense most kids face is paying for college. Even if you still have all of high school ahead of you, your college years will be here before you know it. If you haven't started saving for your education, now is the time to start. Of course, you don't have to use a traditional IRA for this purpose. Two different types of savings plans are made specifically for paying for college.

Your parents may have already opened either a 529 college savings plan or an education savings account (ESA) for you when you were younger. If so, they could have put a certain amount of money into this account and simply let it grow, or they might still be contributing to it. The earlier you start an account like this, the more time it has to increase in value. If your parents aren't making regular contributions to your account, you might consider doing so yourself. With these savings programs, you can set up automatic investments that come out of your bank account regularly. In fact, the

Prepaid Tuition Plan	College Savings Plan
Locks in tuition prices at eligible public and private colleges and universities.	No lock on college costs.
All plans cover tuition and mandatory fees only. Some plans allow you to purchase a room and board option or excess tuition credits for other qualified expenses.	Covers all "qualified higher education expenses," including: tuition, room and board, mandatory fees, books, and computer (if required).
Most plans set lump sum and installment payments prior to purchase based on age of beneficiary and number of years of college tuition purchased.	Many plans have contribution limits in excess of $200,000.
Many states plans guaranteed or backed by state.	No state guarantee. Most investment options are subject to market risk. Your investment may not make any profit or even decline in value.
Most plans have age/grade limit for beneficiary.	No age limits. Open to adults and children.
Most state plans require either owner or beneficiary of plan to be a state resident.	No residency requirement. However, nonresidents may only be able to purchase some plans through financial advisers and brokers.
Most plans have limited enrollment period.	Enrollment open all year.

There are advantages and disadvantages to both prepaid tuition plans and college savings plans. Knowing where you want to go to school can be a big help in deciding which type of plan is better for you. If you aren't sure, a college savings plan may be the way to go.

money in both 529s and ESAs is typically invested in stocks and bonds—much like mutual funds. You might even think of these investments as mutual funds with a specific purpose.

Both college savings plans and retirement savings plans also offer another important benefit. Each one offers certain tax advantages. In most cases you won't pay taxes on the money you invest in these savings plans. One exception is a Roth IRA. With this investment you won't get any tax breaks now, but you will get a huge one when it comes time for retirement. Most retirement savings plans allow you to invest pre-tax dollars, but you will pay taxes on the money you withdraw from these accounts when you retire. This might be an advantage if you will be in a lower tax bracket when you retire. But if your income is low today and you are paying 15 percent income tax, you may not save very much by investing in a traditional IRA. If you invest in a Roth IRA, you will have to pay taxes on the income you invest now, but you won't pay a cent on this money when you retire fifty years from now. The money you save then could be much more than what you will pay in taxes now.

Another option for retirement savings is a 401(k). Once you finish your education and start working full time, your company may offer you this type of retirement savings plan. It works very much like a traditional IRA with one major

Saving and Investing Tips and Trivia

If you like the idea of a 401(k), you might be able to convince your parents to make a similar arrangement with you through your allowance. Ask if they would be willing to match the amount of money you save through a 529 college savings program. They just might be impressed enough with your interest in saving for your future to say yes.

exception. Most employers will match your contributions up to a certain limit. Let's say that you make $25,000 a year and want to put 5 percent of that in your 401(k). This would mean that you are saving $1,250 each year. Your employer may match up to 3 percent (or $750) with an additional 100 percent contribution. It might even match another 2 percent ($500) with an additional 50 percent contribution of $250. This would mean that a total of $2,250 is going into your 401(k) each year. In this situation, contributing to a 401(k) is like earning an extra $1,000 each year.

Both college savings plans and retirement savings plans are long-term investments. You can withdraw money from them early, but in most cases you will pay a penalty. Many plans allow investors to withdraw a certain amount of money for specific purposes. You might be able to use this money to pay for education, medical expenses, or the down payment on your first home purchase. In these situations, it may be worth it to use the money you have saved. It is very important, though, that you continue to contribute to your savings plan. Putting as much money as you can into a college or retirement savings plan now helps ensure that you have enough money for all the things you want to do in the future.

Personal Portfolio Summary

- Securities
- Money Market Funds and Cash
- Certificates
- Annuities
- Mutual Funds

Chapter 1. Finding Money to Save

1. Jamie Downey, Boston.com, "Eight Ways to Save $50 Per Month," April 11, 2013. http://www.boston.com/business/personalfinance/managingyourmoney/archives/2013/04/eight_ways_to_s.html

2. Alexandra Sifferlin, *Time*, "Why Families Who Eat Together Are Healthier," April 24, 2012. http://healthland.time.com/2012/04/24/why-families-who-eat-together-are-healthier/

3. Money-Zine, "Roth IRA Funds Calculator." http://www.money-zine.com/Calculators/Retirement-Calculators/Roth-IRA-Funds-Calculator/

Chapter 2. Starting Small

1. FDIC, "Your Insured Deposits: FDIC Insurance Coverage Basics," December 31, 2012. http://www.fdic.gov/deposit/deposits/insured/basics.html

2. TreasuryDirect, "Treasury Reintroduces 30-Year Bond," October 17, 2012. http://www.treasurydirect.gov/indiv/research/articles/res_invest_articles_30yearbondarticle_0106.htm

3. TreasuryDirect, "Minimum Holding Period For Savings Bonds Extended To 12 Months," January 15, 2003. http://www.treasurydirect.gov/news/pressroom/pressroom_comsb12.htm

Chapter 3. Exploring More Savings Options

1. TreasuryDirect, "The Basics of Treasury Securities," September 27, 2012. http://www.treasurydirect.gov/instit/research/faqs/faqs_basics.htm

2. Fidelity.com, "Tax Exempt Investing." https://www.fidelity.com/learning-center/fixed-income-bonds/tax-exempt-investing

Chapter 4. Risks and Rewards

1. US Securities and Exchange Commission, "What Are High-Yield Corporate Bonds?" http://www.sec.gov/investor/alerts/ib_high-yield.pdf

2. Wells Fargo, "Mutual Funds, Stocks and Bonds." https://www.wellsfargo.com/investing/basics/stocks_bonds_mf

Chapter 5. Financing Your Dreams

1. Money-Zine, "Roth IRA Funds Calculator." http://www.money-zine.com/Calculators/Retirement-Calculators/Roth-IRA-Funds-Calculator/

2. Ibid.

Books

Butler, Tamsen. *The Complete Guide to Personal Finance: For Teenagers and College Students*. Ocala, Florida: Atlantic Publishing Group, 2010.

Gardner, David, and Tom Gardner. *The Motley Fool Investment Guide for Teens*. New York: Fireside, 2002.

Kiyosaki, Robert T. *Rich Dad, Poor Dad for Teens: The Secrets About Money—That You Don't Learn in School!* Scottsdale, Arizona: Plata Publishing, 2012.

Works Consulted

Downey, Jamie. "Eight Ways to Save $50 Per Month." Boston. com, April 11, 2013. http://www.boston.com/business/personalfinance/managingyourmoney/archives/2013/04/eight_ways_to_s.html

FDIC. "Your Insured Deposits: FDIC Insurance Coverage Basics." December 31, 2012. http://www.fdic.gov/deposit/deposits/insured/basics.html

Fidelity.com. "Tax Exempt Investing." https://www.fidelity.com/learning-center/fixed-income-bonds/tax-exempt-investing

Holmberg, Joshua. *The Teen's Guide to Personal Finance*. New York: iUniverse, 2008.

Krantz, Matt. *Investing Online for Dummies*. Hoboken, New Jersey: Wiley Publishing, Inc., 2010.

Mladjenovic, Paul. *Stock Investing for Dummies*. Hoboken, New Jersey: Wiley Publishing, Inc., 2009.

Money-Zine. "Roth IRA Funds Calculator." http://www.money-zine.com/Calculators/Retirement-Calculators/Roth-IRA-Funds-Calculator/

Sifferlin, Alexandra. "Why Families Who Eat Together Are Healthier." *Time*, April 24, 2012. http://healthland.time.com/2012/04/24/why-families-who-eat-together-are-healthier/

TreasuryDirect. http://www.treasurydirect.gov/tdhome.htm

TreasuryDirect. "Minimum Holding Period For Savings Bonds Extended To 12 Months." January 15, 2003. http://www.treasurydirect.gov/news/pressroom/pressroom_comsb12.htm

TreasuryDirect. "The Basics of Treasury Securities."
September 27, 2012. http://www.treasurydirect.gov/instit/
research/faqs/faqs_basics.htm

TreasuryDirect. "Treasury Reintroduces 30-Year Bond."
October 17, 2012. http://www.treasurydirect.gov/
indiv/research/articles/res_invest_
articles_30yearbondarticle_0106.htm

US Securities and Exchange Commission. "What Are High-
Yield Corporate Bonds?" http://www.sec.gov/investor/alerts/
ib_high-yield.pdf

Wang, Jim. "Five Reasons Credit Unions Rock." Bankrate.com,
June 9, 2011. http://www.bankrate.com/financing/banking/
5-reasons-credit-unions-rock

Wells Fargo. "Mutual Funds, Stocks and Bonds."
https://www.wellsfargo.com/investing/basics/stocks_bonds_mf

On the Internet

Mint
https://www.mint.com/

SmartyPig
https://www.smartypig.com/

TreasuryDirect Kids
http://www.treasurydirect.gov/kids/kids.htm

compound interest—Interest earned by both the principal and previous interest earned.

debit card—A card that allows the holder to pay for purchases electronically directly from a bank account.

diversify (dih-VUR-suh-feye)—To put money into multiple investments in order to reduce overall risk.

dividend (DIV-i-dend)—A sum of money paid to shareholders from the company's earnings.

invest—To place money into a financial account or other asset with the goal of making a profit.

laddering—Investing in several investments with different maturity dates in order to increase liquidity.

liquid—Easily accessible or convertible into cash.

mature (muh-CHOOR)—To become due for repayment or reach the end of the interest-earning period.

penalty—An amount of money forfeited for violating the terms of an agreement, such as withdrawing money earlier than agreed.

principal—The original amount of money placed in an investment.

secondary market—The realm of investment where previously issued investments are bought and sold.

waive (WEYV)—To give up or refrain from claiming.

yield (YEELD)—The total amount earned from an investment.